GooD BooK

The Holy Bible

ANTHONY L TOBIN

INTRODUCTION

In early 2013, while living in Hong Kong, I received the sad news that my elderly uncle had passed away in the small town of my birth, Rhayader, Powys, Wales, UK, where he had lived most of his life in a house, thought to be more than 300 years old.

Tower House, Bridge Street, Rhayader, Powys, Wales, Uk

I went to Wales for the funeral and in the house, once owned and occupied by my maternal grandparents, found an antique Bible, of a style I had only previously seen in museums. It's large (approx. 32cm x 25cm x 10cm) and leather bound.

At this point I have a confession … I am not a religious person! However, when inspecting my uncle's Bible I was taken with the beauty of the illustrations scattered through the 1,700 brittle pages.

A collection of these images have been professionally and carefully scanned by specialists in Hong Kong to be offered in this easy to handle format for all to admire and enjoy.

Anthony L Tobin

ACKNOWLEDGEMENTS

I would like to take this opportunity to thank George Mihaylov of Hong Kong Imaging for his work and personal attention to this project. His enthusiasm and professional skills in scanning all illustrations were essential in bringing these magnificent artworks to a much wider audience.

And of course a big thank you to my late Uncle Len Jones for preserving the beautiful antique Bible in his home, which he bequeathed to me and my family.

Anthony L Tobin

ILLUSTRATIONS

The beautiful illustrations presented in this publication look wonderful when printed and framed. This is something you can easily do yourself. However, please note that the files used for this ebook are quite low resolution, to keep the file small enough for downloading. But, if you'd like a hi-res (high resolution) file for a special purpose we can send you one for a small fee.

Anthony L Tobin

WARNING

This is a Christian religious publication. If this offends you, too bad. I don't care. I am not a religious person, but I grew up in a Christian country and it is part of my life.

We celebrated Christmas, Easter and Whitsun (the Christian festival of Pentecost, the seventh Sunday after Easter).

We also sang God Save the Queen and hymns at school assembly every morning.

If this offends you ... please close this book and go away ... far away. Christianity is part of my culture and I'm proud of it.

Anthony L Tobin

"AND I SAW ANOTHER ANGEL FLY IN THE MIDST OF HEAVEN, HAVING THE EVERLASTING GOSPEL TO PREACH UNTO THEM THAT DWELL ON THE EARTH. AND TO EVERY NATION, AND KINDRED, AND TONGUE, AND PEOPLE, SAYING WITH A LOUD VOICE, FEAR GOD, AND GIVE GLORY TO HIM; FOR THE HOUR OF HIS JUDGMENT IS COME; AND WORSHIP HIM THAT MADE HEAVEN, AND EARTH, AND THE SEA, AND THE FOUNTAINS OF WATERS." REVELATION XIV. 6, 7.

CHAPTER I.

1 *The creation of heaven and earth, 3 of the light, 6 of the firmament, 9 of the earth separated from the waters, 11 and made fruitful, 14 of the sun, moon, and stars, 20 of fish and fowl, 24 of beasts and cattle, 26 of man in the image of God. 29 Also the appointment of food.*

IN the *a*beginning *b*God created the heaven and the earth.

2 And the earth was without form, and void; and darkness *was* upon the face of the deep. *c*And the Spirit of God moved upon the face of the waters.

3 *d*And God said, *e*Let there be light: and there was light.

4 And God saw the light, that *it was* good: and God divided 1the light from the darkness.

5 And God called the light *f*Day, and the darkness he called Night. 2And the evening and the morning were the first day.

6 ¶ And God said, *g*Let there be a 3firmament in the midst of the waters, and let it divide the waters from the waters.

7 And God made the firmament, *h*and divided the waters which *were* under the firmament from the waters which *were* above the firmament: and it was so.

8 And God called the firmament Heaven. And the evening and the morning were the second day.

9 ¶ And God said, *i*Let the waters under the heaven be gathered together unto one place, and let the dry *land* appear: and it was so.

10 And God called the dry *land* Earth; and the gathering together of the waters called he Seas: and God saw that *it was* good.

BEFORE CHRIST 4004.

a John i. 1, 2; Heb. i. 10.

b Ps. viii. 3; xxxiii. 6; lxxxix. 11, 12; cii. 25; cxxxvi. 5; cxlvi. 6; Isa. xliv. 24; Jer. x. 12; li. 15; Zech. xii. 1; Acts xiv. 15; xvii. 24; Col. i. 16, 17; Heb. xi. 3; Rev. iv. 11; x. 6.

c Ps. xxxiii. 6; Isa. xl. 13, 14.

d Ps. xxxiii. 9.

e 2 Cor. iv. 6.

1 Heb. *between the light and between the darkness.*

f Ps. lxxiv. 16; civ. 20.

2 Heb. *And the evening was, and the morning was.*

g Job xxxvii. 18; Ps. cxxxvi. 5; Jer. x. 12; li. 15.

3 Heb. *expansion.*

h Prov. viii. 28.

i Ps. cxlviii. 4.

j Job xxvi. 10; xxxviii. 8; Ps. xxxiii. 7; civ. 5; cv. 9; cxxxvi. 6; Prov. viii. 29; Jer. v. 22; 2 Pet. iii. 5.

1

EGYPTIAN SYMBOLS OF THE HEAVENS AND THE EARTH

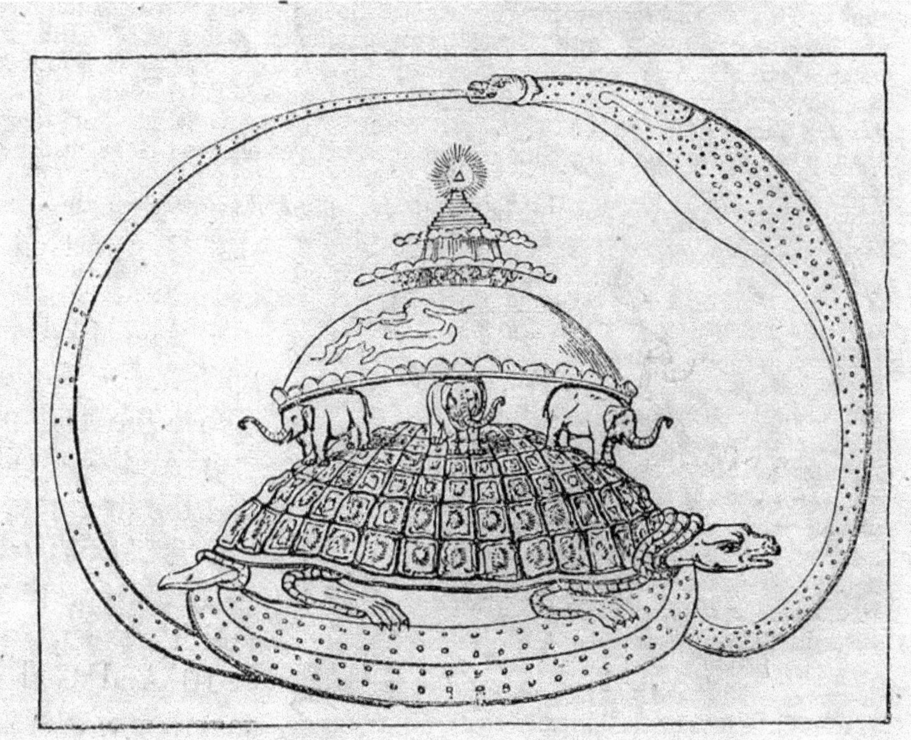

Hindoo Representation of the Universe.

HINDOO REPRESENTATION OF THE UNIVERSE

Egyptian Symbols of the Heavens and the Earth.

REPRESENTATION OF AMMON-KNEPH (THE JUPITER AMMON OF THE GREEKS, FROM KARNAK, IN UPPER EGYPT, A SYMBOL OF BENEVOLENT POWER IN RESPOSE

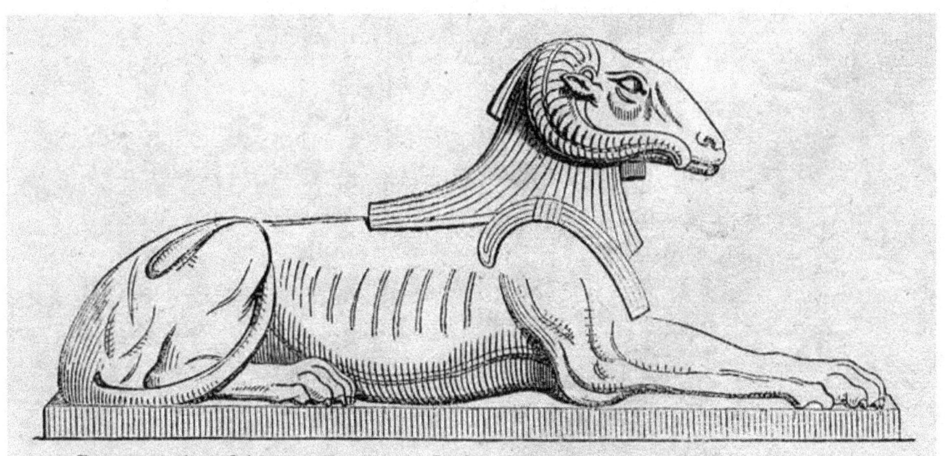

Representation of Ammon-Kneph (the Jupiter Ammon of the Greeks), from Karnak, in Upper Egypt, a symbol of benevolent power in repose.

ISLE OF KISHM, IN THE PERSIAN GULF

Isle of Kishm, in the Persian Gulf

ADAM AND EVE IN EDEN

ADAM AND EVE IN EDEN.

DEATH OF ABEL

THE FIRST MUSICAL INSTRUMENT

ENTERING THE ARK

ENTERING THE ARK.

THE DELUGE

THE ARK AT REST

NOAH'S SACRIFICE

NOAH'S SACRIFICE.

THE CONFUSION
OF TONGUES

SARAH TAKEN INTO PHARAOH'S HOUSE

SARAH TAKEN INTO PHARAOH'S HOUSE.

MELCHIZEDEK BLESSES ABRAM

TEMPLE OF IPSAMBUL

TEMPLE OF IPSAMBUL.

SEPARATION OF ABRAM AND LOT

SEPARATION OF ABRAM AND LOT.

ABRAHAM AND THE THREE ANGELS

THE DESTRUCTION OF SODOM AND GOMORRAH

THE DESTRUCTION OF SODOM AND GOMORRAH.

ABIMELECH RESTORING SARAH TO ABRAHAM

HAGAR AND ISHMAEL CAST FORTH

ABRAHAM OFFERING ISAAC

ABRAHAM AND THE SONS OF HETH

ABRAHAM'S SERVANT AND REBEKAH AT THE WELL

ABRAHAM'S SERVANT AND REBEKAH AT THE WELL.

ISAAC MEETING REBEKAH

ESAU GOING FOR VENISON

ESAU GOING FOR VENISON.

ISAAC BLESSING JACOB

ISAAC BLESSING JACOB.

JACOB'S VISION

JACOB'S VISION.

JACOB POURING OIL ON THE STONE

JACOB KEEPING THE FLOCKS OF LABAN

MEETING OF JACOB AND ESAU

MEETING OF JACOB AND ESAU.

RACHEL'S TOMB

ESAU AND HIS FAMILY DEPARTING

JOSEPH'S DREAM

JOSEPH CAST INTO THE PIT

Find more wonderful graphics from this once lost, now found, unique antique Bible, in Part TWO.